SOME PAGES OF MY DIARY

SUJATA GAUTAM

Made with ♥ on the Notion Press Platform
www.notionpress.com

To my mom, who supported and believed in me
whenever i failed in my life.

Contents

Foreword

CHAPTER ONE

Self Obsession:- It is more dangerous than what you think

So, once I had a boyfriend and hardly 3-4 weeks passed of our relationship, then on one evening we were talking and he said to me that he wouldn't be able to marry me because he wants to marry where her mother wants. It made me so annoyed, I was like it was your decision to make me your girlfriend and at that time you told me that we are going to get married, so how can you be like this now? Then the argument got worst and we broke up. That broke me so deeply and I was feeling so hurt because at that time my exams were also going on & it affected my performance. I was like, I am such a fool, why do I allow people to hurt me, why do I believe them, why do I waste my precious time on them?

And then after 1 or 2 days after this event, he texted me in the evening, and then my anger burst upon him which made me say the I words that I should not. I was like "Do you really think that you deserve this love? It's my mistake that I trusted a boy like you, 'Just look at your personality & mine, it is so different you don't even know English?

And I felt so relaxed that I showed him his worth. This is what happens, whenever anybody hurts us or becomes nasty towards us, we want to do the same thing with them which satisfies our ego.

Then the next day, I uploaded a beautiful picture. "of mine, so that he can realize what he have lost with the caption "Common dude hold your heartbeat. I'm just simply fire" , in my story. So that he can realize what he has lost. But after some minutes of uploading it, I realized that it is so bad, hurt makes us so blind, that we don't even realize that still we have some friends and some loved ones who really care about us, your Instagram story is not only viewed by that one guy, so your caption shouldn't only be targeted towards him.

I realized that I become so much self-obsessed and started thinking that materialistic things can provide us happiness.

I realized that we are living in a world where we gave some much importance to good looks & fashion accessories that we think if we are good looking & have a great personality, then we can make any person get attracted towards us. This map gives false confidence in youth.

Today, the youth have become so self-obsessed about their looks, which makes them think like they are great & it allows them to easily hurt & insult other people.

Till now I have never asked him how much he earns and he also never told me on his own. But when I told him in anger that you are an unemployed guy & don't even know English. So at that time answered anxiously that he was not -unemployed & earns Rs.18,000/ month. This made me the question 'What is this I have I done?? I made him so uncomfortable that he revealed the amount of his salary

Can hurt make us go toxic that we lose our tendency of being kind & good?

CHAPTER TWO

Food and Relations

So, this is what I came to understand about relationships in our lives, they are like food, which is very important for us, but if consumed more than required and separate or different from what is required then it can be harmful to us.

Like, when we are eating food, a time comes & or point comes where we feel like we should stop eating now. If we continue to eat after that then we will be able to see some bad consequences of it. And according to me, the same is with relations also. A time comes when we feel complete that yes there is nothing else remaining now. So, at that time we feel totally fulfilled, with that particular relationship, and that's the time we should end it. If we didn't end it there at that time and continue it further without any purpose, then it will certainly prove bad for us so it is very necessary that we take the right steps and right decisions with appropriate action, whenever we feel or need.

CHAPTER THREE

Is it that much bad to take care of your body and looks?

So yes, here I get so much criticized for my look &, figure & body.

People think that I'm very much arrogant because I am a very good-looking & beautiful girl with an amazing personality. I have heard comments on my back like 'She thinks she's something

And recently one guy told me that 'You girls admire external beauty more' and 'You are trapped in consumerism'.

He was like, ' We will get ugly by age so we shouldn't work on our looks, only the soul is going to remain as it is eternal.

And this all started when he send me a pic of his come books in the wardrobe and there were some cosmetic products lying behind them, so I asked him what are these products.

He was like nothing it's aloe vera and hair wash products. To this, I said, 'Ladkiyon ki Nazar cosmetics products ho pehchan hi leti hai'.

And then after that, he did this comment, "Wow proved that you are a girl". I think you admire external beauty more, trapped in consumerism"

I tried to explain to him that no girls don't only admire external beauty. But he didn't.

But yeah, we can't ignore the fact that we girls face these types of comments so much. We are judged and criticized for our own looks. We are criticized for doing makeup, wearing new clothes, heels, etc. People think that we & are trying to prove something, we only admire eternal beauty & we are arrogant about our looks.

But I don't understand that why is it bad to take care of our looks, health, and body. Yes, we all know that our soul is eternal and our body is transcendent but why do you take it as that we should not take care or get concerned about our looks and health?

Why we can't take it as our body is transient, so we should use it to do more and more good work on this planet, and to keep making the best use of it, we need to keep it fit and healthy.

We all have learned that proverb in our school, 'A healthy body leads to a healthy mind'. But still, girls are getting criticized for grooming themselves.

They get criticized for doing makeup, for wearing western dresses, for posting pictures on insta, etc.

We need to understand that grooming ourselves is not a crime, and there's nothing wrong in getting concerned about looks to some extent.

Excess of anything is bad, whether it is beauty, fashion, workout, or anything else.

this is what we are taught in our scriptures also. It is nowhere written that women should not apply makeup, or wear western dresses and heels.

CHAPTER FOUR

Let the mist of love get clear

Once there was a girl sitting with her boyfriend in the garden on a bench, they both were talking with each other and smiling as they were so happy at that time & then the time to depart came, it was their last meeting, they both said bye to each & the girl kept looking at the boy till he disappeared in distance. She sat on that bench for a little thinking about him & a tear fell from her eyes, then she realized that it is too late and now she should go home. So she stood up from the bench & when she turned back, she realises that there are people who were observing them talking departing & her getting emotional. She saw that one of her acquaintance is coming towards her. He said,

"Hello"

She:- 'Hi'

He:- 'How are you doing?'

She:- 'Fine'

He noticed a trail of tear on her cheek & asked

Are you okay? Is everything fine?

She smiled & said, "Ya, I'm Ok & everything is fine."

Sometimes I wonder that, when we are in love, we are so much in the effect of it that we are not able to see anything existing and happening around us, but yes when that love or that person will go away from you, you will be able to see we all those things clearly and you are going find it very funny that why were they not visible to you before?

CHAPTER FIVE

A polite professor

Story 1:-

So it was when I was in the second semester of my graduation, and due to COVID-19, our classes were conducted online. I had a subject called 'Organtuational Behaviour' and I was not interested in studying, thus I was not interacting in the classes, and sometimes if my professor asks me any question I didn't have the answer of that question,

One day when my professor of 'Organisational Behavior' subject asked me a question & I was unable to answer that question then he asked me very politely & surprisingly 'Sujata, you are a brilliant student & you have received amazing grades in this subject, I saw when I was putting marks of all the students, then why are you not interacting in the class?'

And then I smiled but again I didn't have any answer of that question. Hahaha! I know it's funny. But I found it very sweet, that I still remember that moment. It was so overwhelming how sweetly & politely my professor told me to pay attention & interact in class. And yes from then I started studying seriously & interacting in his class.

Story 2:-

So when I was in 3rd semester, we had a subject called "Entrepreneurship? & it was taught by our HOD. We were told to make a 'Business Plan' for our start-up idea and then we have to present that & answer questions asked by faculty allocated to us. There were sub-plans in that business plans like Marketing plan, finance plan, etc

So I made my business plan but I was not able to "complete some tasks of the finance plan, as I found it too difficult. And I didn't want to appear for the viva, as I was so scared that if my examiner asked me any questions related to the financial plan if my examiner asked why I didn't complete the financial plan, etc.

So when the day of viva came, I decided not to go to college & didn't appear for viva. Students were given time of two more days for the viva, on the second day I asked my classmates that, what was asked in the viva, & they were like, it was not very hard, you have to just explain your business plan. Then I asked "Do they view our business plan till the end? To it, they replied that they just have a look at it.

But I was still nervous. We were given one more very extra day to appear for the viva, I gathered some strength & then appeared for viva on the fourth day. First of all, we have to go to our HOD to ask them who is going to take my viva.

So on the fourth day, I went to college & was waiting outside the cabin of my HOD for him, and yes I was still nervous. All of a sudden he came outside, looked at me & smiled. And I got so confused, I didn't know how to react. I asked him about the viva, and he answered that this particular examiner is going to take your viva & you have to reach her at this location. One thing which amazed me was how a smile can let you forget about all your nervousness. And this was the great lesson I learned on that day that, it is very important to keep smiling not only for yourself but also for others as we don't know how & to what extent it can help others. It doesn't only help us feel good, o but others also.

CHAPTER SIX

The basic nature

So it was when I was in 5th standard my summer vacation was going on & my dad's transfer happened at that time, so we have to move to another city. I came to a new city with my family and we were living in a rented house. Barely 2-3 days passed, and when in the evening children play outside their homes & on the road, I used to look at them from my window, I was missing playing with my friends. I alalsoanted to go outside & play with them. When I go to the rooftops of my house I see some children playing there also. I wished deeply to go and play along with them.

But I was new there and didn't know how they are going to react if I approached them. I was not sure if they allow me to play with them or not. So for some more days, I kept looking at them from my window. I was missing how I used to play games and drive a bicycle with my friends, as they were doing.

But then one evening when some children playing on the rooftop, I went there and approached them to make me play along with them. Yes, the rooftops of all the houses of that society were joint. And yes, they allowed me to become part of their group to play along with them. We all become good friends & I was a happy child again. But very lately when I become mature, I understood why there was a deep desire inside me to go outside & play along with those children. Because it is the basic nature of children to play. And it is very important that they do that. Parents should not put restrictions on them to go outside, make friends & play along with them. I know how they feel when they are not able to do or allowed to behave in the way that is their basic nature.